The Shoes of Tanbouyy

BY SHIMON BALLAS

ILLUSTRATED BY ORA EITAN

SABRA BOOKS · NEW YORK

SBN 87631–016–1
LIBRARY OF CONGRESS CATALOG CARD NUMBER 79–82698
PRINTED IN ISRAEL BY E. LEWIN-EPSTEIN LTD., BAT YAM
COPYRIGHT © 1970 AMERICAN-ISRAEL PUBLISHING CO., LTD.

To Avivit

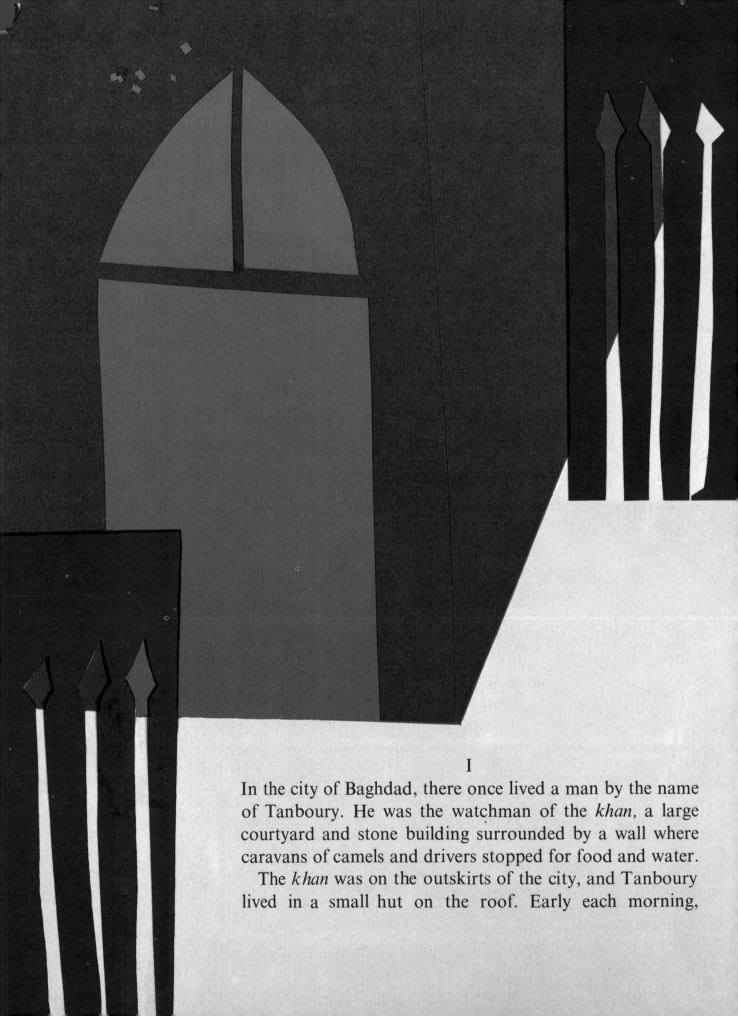

I

In the city of Baghdad, there once lived a man by the name of Tanboury. He was the watchman of the *khan*, a large courtyard and stone building surrounded by a wall where caravans of camels and drivers stopped for food and water.

The *khan* was on the outskirts of the city, and Tanboury lived in a small hut on the roof. Early each morning,

Tanboury would come down and open the gates of the *khan* for the caravans to enter.

He would watch them come in, the camels laden with goods from faraway places across the seas.

Soon the courtyard was filled with noisy men and animals. His work done, Tanboury would go off to an old, crumbling mosque. At the gate were his friends, beggars all, and there they would sit and talk and listen all day long, until the voice of the *muezzin* in the tower called the people to come to the mosque for evening prayers.

This was in the time when the royal Eabas family ruled the land. In Baghdad there were many poor people, but the scribes who wrote the history of the city mentioned only the bravery of the soldiers and the wealth of the noblemen. They said nothing about the poor people except Tanboury. His name was entered into thick books, and his story is still being told.

What is really so unusual about Tanboury's story? Was Tanboury so very different from all other poor people? Was he wiser? Did he work harder? Was he perhaps more foolish or cruel?

No! No! Not at all! He was different *because of his shoes!*

And indeed, his shoes were very odd: large and puffy, like a clumsy, outsized feedbag on a small donkey, but heavy like the millstone that grinds grain, and covered with patches of every shape and color, all worn and faded. These worn and faded shoes had served Tanboury for many, many years, and should really have been thrown into the trash a long time ago.

But Tanboury was poor, and he had no money for new shoes. He kept on repairing his old ones, patching them with scraps of leather and bits of cloth. He kept them from falling apart by tying them with bits of string or rope that he picked up in the gutter.

And so the shoes grew larger, heavier, until they had no shape at all. Nothing could possibly look as coarse and ugly

3

as Tanboury's shoes, everyone agreed. It got so that the people of Baghdad used to say about a pesty person: "He's a bigger nuisance than Tanboury's shoes!"

Tanboury was not happy to hear such words spoken about *his* shoes. He did not run after honors nor did he especially want to hear people say good things about him, but what they said about his shoes caused him much pain.

He longed for the day when he would be rid of them. He would sit in his little hut and wonder how long he would have to save his pennies before he could afford the price of a new pair of shoes—and perhaps a new coat as well, instead of the old, torn one that he wore. Tanboury kept his coins in a small bundle, under his pillow. He counted them every night, his heart singing for joy as their number continued to grow.

None of his idle friends knew what he was planning, for Tanboury was afraid that they would poke fun at him.

"Look at that Tanboury!" he could hear them say. "He has gone mad! He saves money by going hungry, just to buy a pair of shoes!" Then everyone would laugh and jeer at him: "Why don't you go to the rich people and ask them for a pair of old shoes? If you eat any less than you are eating now, you will starve!"

Yes, Tanboury could have gotten a pair of old shoes from one of the merchants who stopped at the *khan,* but he did not dream of asking them. He was poor but he was proud. He was not the wisest man in the world, but neither was he a fool. Yet it should be remembered that he became famous because of his shoes.

Many long days did Tanboury toil until he had saved enough money for a pair of shoes. When the great day came, he took his bundle of coins and hurried to the shoe market, still without telling his friends what he was up to. And it is really on this day that the story of Tanboury's strange shoes begins.

II

In one of the stalls of the shoe market, Tanboury saw a pair of bright red shoes that he liked immediately. Luckily, the price was not more than the money in his bundle; in fact, there were even a few pennies left over.

Grinning with joy, Tanboury put his new shoes on and walked a few steps to see how they felt. Wonderful! He felt almost weightless, as if he were floating on air, they were that comfortable.

He hurried from the shoe stall, skipping along the market place like a young boy.

At first he thought he would go straight to the mosque and show his new shoes to his friends. But then his eyes rested on the old pair that he was still carrying, and he said to himself:

"This is no way for me to appear before my friends, in my shiny red shoes, but still holding this ugly old pair. I will get rid of them first, before I go to the mosque. But how? Throw them away on a pile of rubbish? They may still be good for somebody's tired feet. It would be better to sell them to someone who has no shoes at all. That way, he would have a pair of shoes and I'd have a few more pennies."

Tanboury hurried off to the Second-Hand Things Market, and there he stood, offering his old shoes for sale. He waited all day long, but not a single buyer appeared. Towards evening, long after the *muezzin* had called the people to come to the mosque, a man from the desert, barefoot and dressed in rags, came to the market place. He walked slowly, shuffling along from one stall to the next, peering at the shelves.

"Here! I have shoes, strong and cheap!" Tanboury called out to him.

The man came closer, looked at the shoes, tested their weight in his hands, turned them this way and that, and then said hoarsely:

"Too worn."

"Ha! Come, my dear fellow," cried Tanboury. "These

shoes were made when cobblers could still be depended on. They have served me well for many years, and they are still good for bare feet."

The man from the desert looked the shoes over once again, and again turned them from side to side, then put them on his big coarse feet and walked a few paces, back and forth. "They are heavy, very heavy," he grumbled.

"But they are thick and warm," said Tanboury eagerly. "In the cold of the night they will keep your feet warm. In the daytime they will keep out the hot sand. They will protect your feet from snakes and scorpions and all the other dangers of the desert."

Again the man from the desert paced back and forth in the shoes, trying to make up his mind. Tanboury in the meanwhile kept on chattering about how good and how cheap the shoes were. At last the man agreed to buy the shoes if Tanboury would lower the price. Tanboury reduced the cost of the shoes by a few pennies, then a few more, until at last the two agreed. The man handed Tanboury the money, took the shoes and went off, as Tanboury showered the blessing of Allah and Mohammed on him.

Tanboury returned to the *khan,* very pleased with himself. It was now evening and the yard was empty. Tanboury locked the gate and went up to his hut on the roof. He lit a candle, took off his new shoes and placed them by the door. The flame of the candle shone on the sparkling red shoes. In Tanboury's eyes there was a gleam of happiness such as only a poor person can feel, once in a great while. Tanboury sat down on his rickety bed and ate his supper: a crust of dry bread, a chunk of cheese and a handful of dates. He washed it down with water from a covered pitcher. Not for a moment did he take his eyes off his new shoes.

His poor meal seemed like a feast. He thought about his friends at the mosque. Ah, how their eyes would open wide

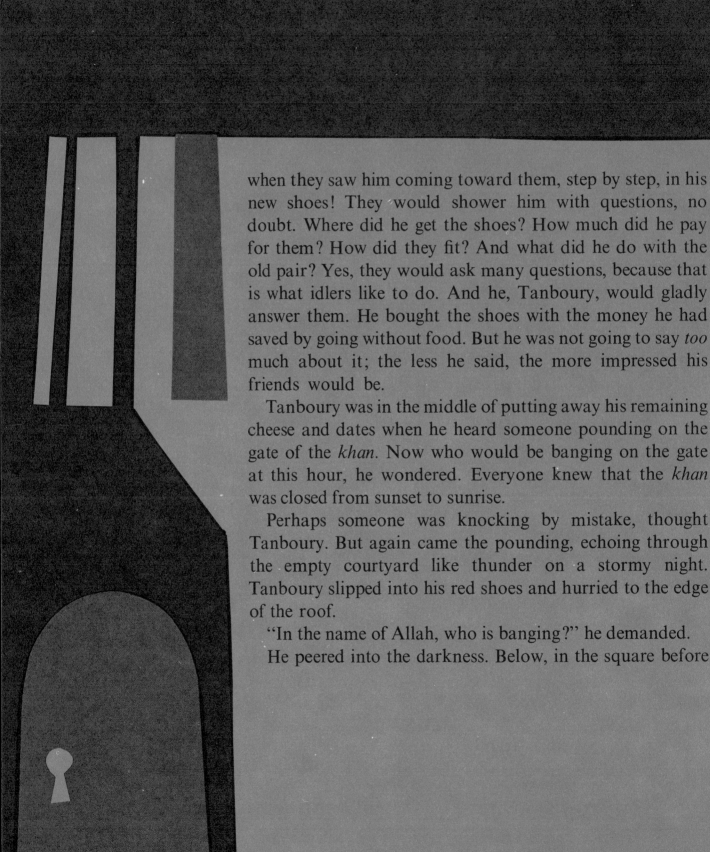

when they saw him coming toward them, step by step, in his new shoes! They would shower him with questions, no doubt. Where did he get the shoes? How much did he pay for them? How did they fit? And what did he do with the old pair? Yes, they would ask many questions, because that is what idlers like to do. And he, Tanboury, would gladly answer them. He bought the shoes with the money he had saved by going without food. But he was not going to say *too* much about it; the less he said, the more impressed his friends would be.

Tanboury was in the middle of putting away his remaining cheese and dates when he heard someone pounding on the gate of the *khan*. Now who would be banging on the gate at this hour, he wondered. Everyone knew that the *khan* was closed from sunset to sunrise.

Perhaps someone was knocking by mistake, thought Tanboury. But again came the pounding, echoing through the empty courtyard like thunder on a stormy night. Tanboury slipped into his red shoes and hurried to the edge of the roof.

"In the name of Allah, who is banging?" he demanded.

He peered into the darkness. Below, in the square before

the gate where travelers tied up their animals after unloading their wares, he could make out the figures of two men. One was clutching the other by the scruff of the neck.

"Hey, Tanboury, are you asleep?" he yelled.

Tanboury recognized the voice of Ahmed, the guard. "What is wrong, Ahmed?" he cried. "What has happened?"

"So! You were asleep!" Ahmed yelled back. "And here I have caught the thief who stole your shoes while you were snoring!"

Tanboury clasped his head in amazement. "What thief?" he called back. "What are you talking about?"

"He tried to get past the city gates, but I was right there," boasted Ahmed. "He tucked your shoes under his arm and began running like a deer, but I caught up with him!"

"But Ahmed!" cried Tanboury. "He bought the shoes from me!"

"What! You sold your shoes?"

"That's right. I sold the shoes to him in the market. He paid me. He's not a thief. Why didn't you ask him how he got the shoes?"

"He told me that he had bought them, but who believes a good-for-nothing like this? Now tell me, are you going to go around barefoot?"

"I bought a new pair," replied Tanboury, proudly.

"A new pair? Well, may they bring you good luck," said Ahmed. He let go of the man from the desert. "And here I was so sure.." he added in disappointment. Then he

9

remembered how he had caught the supposed thief. This amused him a great deal and he went off to his post at the city gates, whistling.

As soon as Ahmed had gone, the man from the desert called up to Tanboury: "Give me back my money! Give me back my money and take back your shoes! They are the shoes of the devil himself! Take them!" With this, he flung the shoes up to the rooftop, one after the other. One shoe sailed past Tanboury's head and the other hit him on the shoulder.

"Give me back my money! Give me back my money!" the man below kept on yelling.

Tanboury was so taken aback that he could not utter a single word. He stumbled back to the hut, took three coins out from his bundle, and threw them down to the man, who was still yelling: "They are the shoes of the devil! They are the shoes of the devil!" A moment later he disappeared into the darkness.

Tanboury stood on the roof and gazed at his old shoes, lying before him like two dead hulks. Things had happened so quickly that his mind could not absorb it all. The joy that had filled his heart was gone, and he grew more and more upset. His heavy, ugly shoes were back with him once more, and now no one would want to buy them. He could not even *give* them away as a present, since poor people do not give things away. And if they were to remain in the hut, he would feel sad every time he looked at them.

What was he to do? Here he had thought that buying new shoes and getting rid of the old pair would stop people from talking about him and his ugly shoes. And now he was burdened with them perhaps forever!

The more Tanboury thought about the shoes, the more hopeless did everything seem to be. He could not sleep. He

kept tossing and turning until, just before dawn, a wonderful idea came to him. He tied the old shoes into a bundle, left the *khan,* and hurried to the banks of the Tigris River, which flows through the middle of Baghdad—even today boats and rafts glide along its waters, and poor women go there to do their laundry.

When Tanboury reached the river, it was still dark. Only the lapping of the waves could be heard. He looked about to make sure that no one was watching, then heaved the bundle as far into the river as he could. The shoes hit the water with a mighty splash and sank at once. Tanboury stood there until he was sure that the shoes were gone and would never, never come up again. He turned away with a happy chuckle. Now he would go straight to the mosque and enjoy the admiration of his friends.

We shall let Tanboury go on to the mosque, in his new red shoes, while we go back to the Tigris River. Something is going on there; yes, there's a boat out there on the water. In the boat there is a fisherman. We watch him as he casts his line into the water, but all that he seems to be catching are small fish, which he throws into a reed basket by his side. But now . . . ah! the hook at the end of his strong line must have caught a big one! We see the fisherman's face. It is all smiles as he hauls in the taut line. Slowly the catch comes to the surface: a shapeless bundle, heavy and wrapped in rags.

The fisherman's jaw drops with disappointment, but then a thought comes to him: perhaps this is an ancient treasure! With trembling fingers, he unties the knot and opens the bundle. A pair of old shoes! Thoroughly disgusted, the fisherman is about to toss them back into the water when suddenly he recognizes them.

"By Allah!" he says to himself. "Why, these are Tanboury's shoes! He must have bathed in the river, and the waves washed the shoes away from the shore. They must surely be returned to him, for he is poor and cannot afford to buy a new pair."

And so the fisherman puts the shoes down in the boat and keeps on fishing. Around noon, finished with his fishing, he stops off at the *khan*. Tanboury is not to be seen. The fisherman, pleased with himself, goes up to the hut on the roof and leaves the shoes at Tanboury's door. How great will be Tanboury's joy when he returns and finds his shoes!

The fisherman feels happy because of the good deed he has done, but he has no idea how much grief it is to bring to poor Tanboury. When the watchman of the *khan* returns from the mosque, highly pleased by what his friends had to say about his new shoes, the first thing he sees at the door of his hut is his old ugly shoes. They seem to be grinning cruelly. Tanboury almost faints.

How could they have floated up and out of the river and onto the roof? Why, he had thrown them far into the Tigris, with his own hands! He had seen them sink, with his own eyes! Poor Tanboury! How is he to know that his friend the fisherman is the cause of it all?

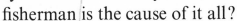

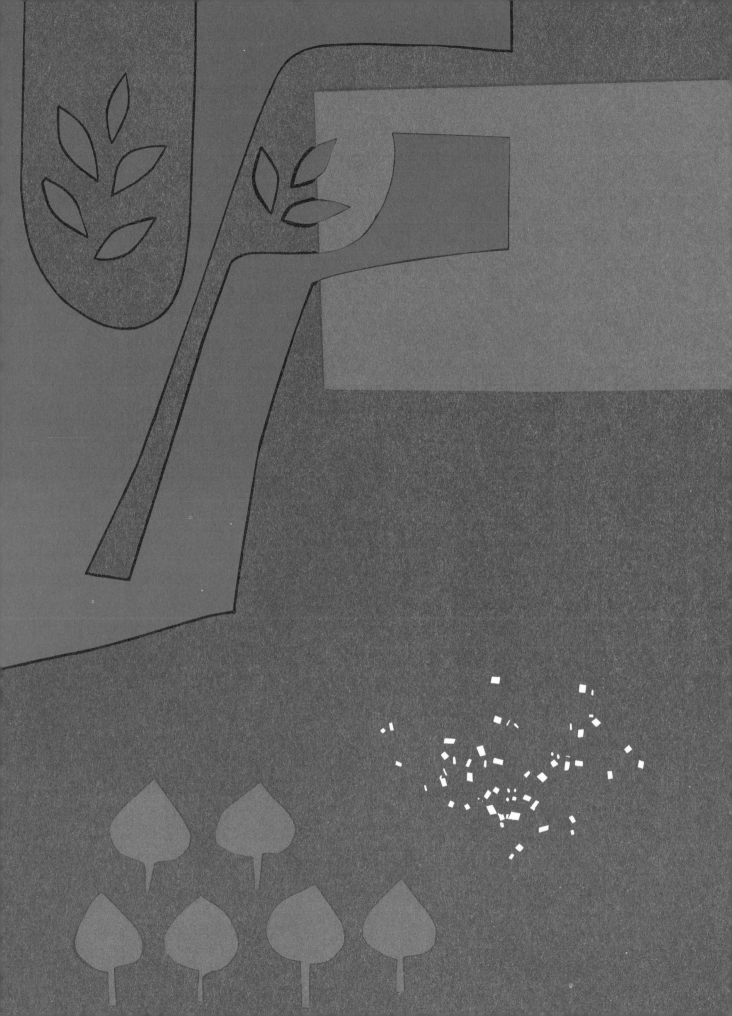

III

All night, Tanboury lay awake, racking his brain for a way out of his nightmare. At dawn, his old shoes tucked firmly under his arm, he left the *khan* and headed toward the West Gate. At that point, the canal that carried off the sewage of Baghdad ran right along the wall. The banks of the canal were covered with heaps of refuse and trash. Tanboury flipped his shoes onto the nearest heap and hurried away, as if someone were following him.

He did not see the shoes roll down the slope of the rubbish heap, straight into the canal waters.

But that was not all. Not only did the shoes themselves roll down but, in doing so, they loosened a solid pile of trash, large enough to clog the narrow canal and make a dam of it. The sewage water began to rise, and soon it overflowed the bank, forming puddles, then spreading out into a slimy marsh until it broke through an embankment. This embank-

15

ment surrounded the garden belonging to Abu Alillah, one of the wealthiest men in Baghdad . . . At this point, let us shut our eyes and ears lest we see and hear Abu Alillah, as the foul smell of the overflow hits his nostrils and the dirty water courses, in front of his staring eyes, among his roses and lilies and jasmin, covering his green lawns and ruining his entire garden.

Without wasting another moment, Abu Alillah ordered his servants to trace the ill-smelling flood to its source, while he himself mounted his horse and galloped to the spot. When he saw that the trouble began at the sewage canal, he became very angry. He turned his horse around and spurred it toward the Governor's mansion. Abu Alillah was a man of importance in the Caliph's court and he was going to tell the Governor, without mincing words, what he thought of the way the canal was being drained, and demand that the matter be taken care of at once.

The Governor was in the large guest hall of the mansion, surrounded by his friends and servants. This made no difference to Abu Alillah. He stormed into the hall and began shouting. His bitter words about the smelly sewage, uttered in front of all the guests—so enraged the Governor that he turned almost purple. When he was at last able to control himself, the Governor said:

"My canals are in perfect working order, and never have I received a single complaint about them. If something did go wrong with the canal near your garden, I shall order my laborers to go there at once, and they will deal with the trouble." With this, he ordered his head servant to send a crew of canal workers to the trouble spot. More than that, he rose, excused himself, and rode with Abu Alillah to the canal.

The Governor's laborers and Abu Alillah's servants went into the canal up to their knees, and set about bringing up from the bottom rags and stones, rubbish and broken branches, until one of them came up with Tanboury's shoes. Immediately the water broke through and flowed down the canal in a lively stream. The Governor and Abu Alillah, still mounted upon their horses, stared at the huge shoes which had clogged the canal, as their men cheered.

Suddenly someone cried: "Why, these are the shoes of Tanboury!"

Of course! Was there anyone in Baghdad who did *not* know them?

The Governor's face now grew red with anger. He ordered his men to arrest the criminal who dared throw away his shoes in a public place and cause such grief to so important a person! Then he turned to Abu Alillah and said: "You see, do you not, dear sir, that there is nothing wrong with my canals? All the evil you have suffered came from the owner of these horrible shoes. I shall see to it that he is punished, lest he give our city a bad name in other parts of the kingdom. He shall be punished as harshly as the law allows!"

Having said this, the Governor bade farewell to Abu Alillah and returned to his guests at the mansion. Abu Alillah went back to his garden, happy that the foul flood was gone but sad indeed over the damage done to his beautiful garden.

Now let us hurry back to Tanboury. Having gotten rid of his old shoes—so he thought—he ambled off to the mosque. Surrounded by his friends, he recounted the story of his old shoes and their return to his hut, much to the delight of his listeners. Tanboury, usually among the listeners (or, at most, a questioner), suddenly found himself, for the second day in a row, the spinner of marvelous tales. First, he had bought new shoes and was able to sell his old ones, and now there was the wonderful story of how his famous shoes had come back to him, once from the market place and again from the bottom of the Tigris.

He was in the middle of telling the story, for the third time, with his listeners wide-eyed, hanging on his every word, when the Governor's men arrived with orders to arrest him. Tanboury's friends were stricken with fright at sight of the authorities and fled in all directions. Tanboury remained, trembling, rooted to the spot, and quite unable to understand what the Governor's men wanted of him. They gave him no chance to ask. They quickly tied a noose around his neck and dragged him along, as one would drag a stubborn calf or a hardened criminal.

Even when Tanboury was brought before the Governor, he did not have the slightest idea of what he was accused. The Governor, fuming over the harsh words that he had been forced to listen to from Abu Alillah, was waiting for Tanboury in order to loose his wrath on the luckless watchman. And indeed, as soon as Tanboury's foot crossed the threshold, the Governor broke into a string of oaths, curses and threats that made Tanboury's hair stand on end. The Governor did not let up until he grew hoarse and was finally seized with a coughing fit.

Poor Tanboury just stood there, head bowed, not daring to ask why he was being treated to such a long string of curses. He didn't really know how long he stood there, under the shower of oaths; all he knew was that every minute seemed like a year. It did take some time, for the Governor was a learned man and could handle words very well. Besides, he insisted on repeating each curse at least twenty times, until the bitterness in his heart began to recede. All this took time and eventually Tanboury, being blessed with a pair of good ears, gathered that at the root of the curses and even of his arrest was his pair of old shoes. He was still trying to figure out what it was that his shoes could possibly have done, when the Governor ordered him flogged twenty times.

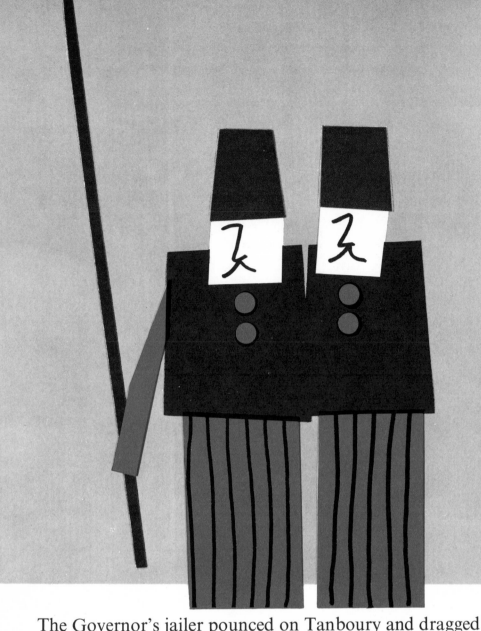

The Governor's jailer pounced on Tanboury and dragged him off to the courtyard, where he was stripped of his clothes and whipped with a wet leather strap that left a welt on his skin with each blow. Tanboury gritted his teeth and didn't allow a single sound to escape his lips. He knew that no amount of screaming would do him any good; if anything, it would anger the Governor even more. In his heart there was just one prayer: after the flogging, Almighty Allah, let there be no more ranting and raving.

His prayer was fulfilled. The guards returned his garments to him and allowed him to go. But he had not taken two steps, when "blip, blop!"—his dirty old shoes came flying at him, like stones thrown at a mad dog.

"Take your treasure with you," yelled the jeering guards.

For a moment Tanboury stared at the guards and tears

came to his eyes. It was not enough that they had flogged him! Now they were laughing at his misery. He wanted to run away and leave the shoes there, but he thought better of it. The guards might become angry and haul him back for more flogging, and poor Tanboury had had enough. With a deep sigh, he picked up the shoes and went his way.

Where should he go with them? Back to the hut? Or should he again throw them into the gutter? Those cursed shoes had been following him like a shadow, as though they wanted to take away all his joy in the new pair. It was bad enough when he was still wearing the old shoes and the people had laughed at him. It was bad enough he had had to save pennies and go hungry in order to be able to buy a new pair. But now the old shoes had caused him to be flogged, like a common criminal! Surely somewhere in this great and mighty city there was some way of getting rid of the shoes. And why was everyone so ready to bring them back to him? Why shouldn't he, Tanboury, have the same right as everyone else to throw away an old pair of shoes, if he wanted to? Everyone, even his old friends at the mosque, had expected him to wear his old shoes forever.

Tanboury kept on walking, bitterness in his heart and anger in his soul. Without noticing where he was going, he found himself in Baghdad's richest neighborhood, where mansions, centered about a huge round courtyard stood in the midst of blossoming gardens. A fountain surrounded by stately palm trees shot gleaming streams of water into the air. In the peaceful noon hour, the mansions in the courtyard seemed asleep.

The sweet scent of perfume and flowers came to Tanboury's nose, and the sounds that came to his ears were most pleasant : the quiet hissing of the water from the fountain, the cooing of doves high in the trees, the twittering of birds and the gentle flapping of their wings. Strangely enough, there was not a soul in sight and not a sound of any human being anywhere— the perfect moment to sit down in the shade of the trees, away from the noisy market place, always filled with shouts and quarreling.

But Tanboury was in no mood for all this. His body was twisted from the bruises caused by the flogging and his limbs were shaking with anger. He stopped and glared at the trees

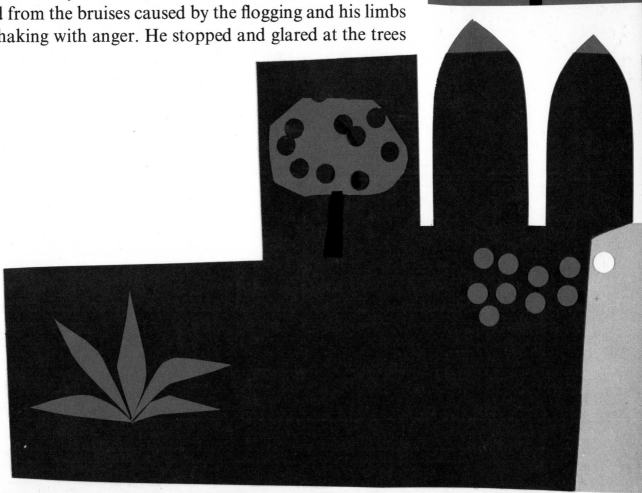

and the mansions, and within him burned the flame of revenge. He who had never done anything evil to anyone was now set upon by everybody! His hand, the one holding the shoes, began to swing back and forth until, with a mighty heave, he let go of the pair. The shoes flew upward, like a stone from a sling, high above the courtyard. They cleared the trees and landed, like a shooting star, on the roof of one of the mansions.

Three cheers for Tanboury! What a fellow! He had never served in the Caliph's army and had no training in throwing on target, but here he was able to land a perfect bull's-eye. Think of that! What Tanboury had thrown was not a ball or a spear or a smooth stone, or even an ordinary shoe, but his clumsy old shoes, tied together with string, looking like two horses tied together by their tails. They could have landed in one of the trees, or even in the fountain, but they landed on a roof, just as Tanboury had hoped.

Now, why *did* Tanboury want his ugly old shoes to land on the roof of the mansion? Well, the people of Baghdad who were familiar with Tanboury's shoes were the poor and simple folk, the fisherman, the guard at the gate, the laborer who cleaned the canal. But not the rich people, and certainly not anyone who owned a mansion! Now do you understand? Even if the owner of the mansion himself would find the shoes on the roof, all he would do would be to order one of his servants to throw them away—and that would be that!

Anyway, the sight of his shoes landing on the roof of the mansion pleased Tanboury very much. Now he was rid of them forever. Let them lie there, on the roof! Let them rot in the sun, right above the heads of the rich! A feeling of happiness came over Tanboury. His bruises no longer hurt so much. He left the courtyard and turned his steps toward the *khan*.

Let us allow him to go in peace, but we shall remain here, in the shadow of one of the trees. Something unusual will happen here in a few hours. Until then, we shall have to be patient.

Now, as we know, it was noon when Tanboury came to the neighborhood. The people living in the mansions were taking their noon-hour nap. They are not like other people—the shopkeepers and artisans, farmhands and porters and blacksmiths, all those who have to work hard and who go to bed early at night in order to get up early in the morning.

People who live in mansions never go to bed early, and therefore they must take a nap at noon. The people living in the mansion on whose roof Tanboury had thrown his shoes were so soundly asleep that they did not even hear the loud thud they made as they landed. Not even the servants nor the watchmen nor the dogs were aroused.

The noon-hour departed and evening drew near. From the minaret of the mosque came the cry of the *muezzin*, calling to prayer. The people in the mansions slowly opened their eyes and rose from their couches. One of them, who happened to be a member of the Caliph's family and a man of property, at once grew very busy. A fine party was going to be held at his mansion that night, to which he had invited the generals of the army and many important men of Baghdad.

And a fine party it was! An orchestra played beautiful music, singers sang lovely songs and dancers performed gracefully, as the guests clapped their hands in delight. The large courtyard, empty when Tanboury was there, was now crowded with men and animals. Carriages drew up to the door, one after another. Sleek horses stood tied to the fence posts, and well-kept dogs moved about, sniffing and barking, just to show that they, too, were important. Inside the mansion the servants were hard at work, moving from one table to another, from one couch to the next, filling plates and glasses as soon as they were emptied. Some food was also brought out to the courtyard for the footmen and the coachmen and the guards, and also fodder was provided for the horses and fine table scraps for the dogs.

Inside the wall of the mansion, a path led around to the servants' entrance and to the giant kitchen. From the fire-place, where the meat was being roasted, came mouth-watering smells that spread to the air outside. The chief cook, a heavy man in a spotless white coat, directed the kitchen and kept telling the other cooks what to do.

Well, we are not interested in the chief cook or his helpers. We want to know more about this gathering of cats that we see near the doorway, huddled together and meowing loudly. Every once in a while one of the cooks would come dashing out of the kitchen, broom in hand, and scatter the cats in all directions. But cats are stubborn creatures; no sooner are they chased away than back they come, meowing and wailing and begging.

And so they stood there, the pupils of their sharp eyes following every move made by the cooks inside, their bodies crouching and ready to dart into the kitchen to make off with anything into which they could sink their teeth (except the legs of the cooks, of course). But the cooks were on the look-out. They charged the cats with huge ladles and hot spits. At one time the cats actually got into the kitchen and hid behind one of the big pots, but this time they were seen by the chief cook himself. He immediately shouted to his helpers, and again the poor cats were driven out, as hungry as before.

All except one cat. This one was so frightened that he lost his senses completely. Instead of escaping to the garden outside as did all the other cats, he scrambled around the pots and suddenly found himself at the foot of a long, steep flight of dark stairs. Without another thought, he streaked up the stairs. None of the cooks had seen him, because all of them had rushed to the garden to chase the other cats. If this cat had had any sense, he could have remained in the kitchen, alone, and had a picnic. But, no, our cat kept on speeding up the stairs until he came to the roof. There he sat down to rest and to wait until things had quieted down below. Of course, the thought that he would have to make his way through the kitchen and past all the cooks didn't make him happy at all. He decided that he would have to wait on the roof, all by himself, until the party was over and the cooks gone.

Suddenly the cat's sharp eyes came to rest on something big and clumpy, right in the center of the roof. To the cat it seemed that this strange object was about to pounce on him. The poor creature almost died of fright on the spot. His back humped, his hair stood on end, and his claws tried to dig into the tiles on the roof, ready to meet the worst. Then, seeing that this thing made no move, the cat began to lose some of his fear; perhaps it's just a bad dream, he thought. He blinked once, twice, three times, then opened his eyes wide. No, the thing was still there, as big as ever.

By this time our cat had forgotten all about the kitchen and the cooks. This new thing had to be dealt with right away. The cat gathered up his courage and took a step toward it. Now he tried to learn more about it by using his sense of smell. He sniffed, and his nose twitched; the smell wasn't very good. The thing didn't move. The cat waited another minute and took another step. Nothing happened.

And now the cat was only one leap away. He peered at it again, but now he was sure that it was harmless. He drew himself as taut as a bowstring, crouched, then leaped forward and sank his teeth into the object. Well, one thing was sure— it wasn't a mouse, only something heavy and tough and hard as a rock. The cat tried to sink his teeth into it deeper—and almost broke them. He pushed the shoes over (of course we know that the "thing" was Tanboury's old shoes), looking for a softer spot. Finding none, he became very angry and began wrestling with them, until both cat and shoes were very close to the edge of the roof. The cat stopped barely in time to save himself from rolling off, but Tanboury's shoes plunged down to the garden below just as one of the guests passed the spot.

The shoes landed right on the head of the luckless guest. And who was he? Almighty Allah, none other than our old friend, Abu Alillah himself!

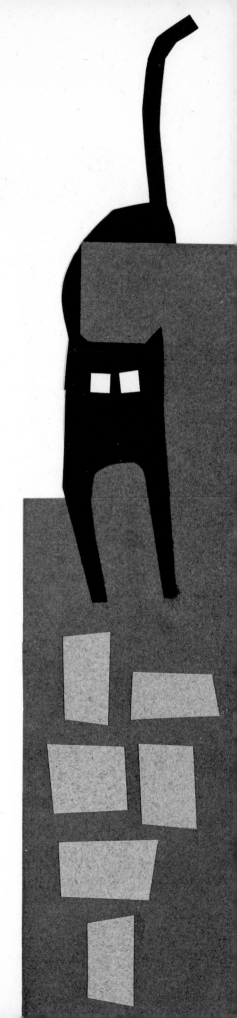

V

How can anyone possibly describe the uproar in the mansion the moment that Abu Alillah, reeling from the blow on his head, let out a cry that could be heard well up the Tigris River! Panic broke out among the guests. They thought that the walls were coming down or, worse still, that the Caliph's enemies had fallen upon the city. Even the guards began running away like chaff before the wind. Abu Alillah lay on the ground, holding his shiny head on which a lump the size of a hen's egg was already forming.

The host of the mansion was inside when the shoes fell, but, hearing the awful bellowing, he rushed out to see what had happened. By this time Abu Alillah was surrounded by a host of people, some trying to help him by squeezing the lump on his head to make it smaller. This only caused Abu Alillah more pain, and he shrieked like a bull at the slaughter. Then someone remembered that the Caliph's own doctor was among the guests and ran off to get him, as all the others began calling for the doctor loudly by name.

What could have happened to him? Like many of the other guests, he had left the mansion in panic but he did not head for the garden. Instead, he ran straight to his carriage in the courtyard, ready to climb aboard and speed away. Now that he heard his name called, he hurried back, shamefacedly. The people made way for him. He came close to

Abu Alillah, looked at the bump on his head, and told them all not to worry: Abu Alillah would live.

Now Abu Alillah, happy to learn that he was not going to die from the blow, slowly rose to his feet and staggered back into the mansion. The musicians were standing idly by and Abu Alillah, eager to show the others that he was a jolly good fellow, ordered them to play. At the sound of the music, everything returned to normal. The servants brought more food and drink, the dancers swirled about, and the accident to Abu Alillah was all but forgotten.

All this time, no one thought of looking for the thing that had landed on Abu Alillah's head. Tanboury's shoes lay in the garden, unseen under a jasmin bush. Now any other pair

of old shoes would either have rotted there or else a servant would have found them and thrown them into the rubbish pile. But shoes as big and queer as Tanboury's cannot be gotten rid of so easily.

The very next day, the gardener came along to take care of the plants which the guests of the night before had trampled in their excitement. The first thing he saw, under the jasmin bush, was the pair of patchwork shoes. He recognized them at once.

"What would Tanboury's shoes be doing *here?*" he wondered. "Can it be that he was a guest at the party? But that's ridiculous! Perhaps he came here with the other beggars and idlers, for whatever scraps of food the guests had left, whatever had not been given to the dogs. But Tanboury was no beggar. Perhaps he came to steal? But then, Tanboury is not a thief. And yet, only someone in a big hurry would leave his shoes behind."

The gardener lost no time. He went straight to the owner of the mansion and told him what he had found. When the owner heard the story, he went pale and his eyes almost popped out of his head. "Why, those shoes almost killed Abu Alillah," he gasped. He ordered his stable boy to saddle a horse and off he galloped to see the Governor of the city. The gall of that scoundrel, climbing to the roof and pelting the guests with shoes!

Well, let us not dwell on the sad story of the hunt for Tanboury and how he was dragged from the old mosque to the Governor again. Let us not seek to know what harsh and unpleasant words the Governor had for the luckless watchman of the *khan*. It is enough to say that once more Tanboury had to undergo the same torture—except that this time he was given thirty lashes and the Governor sent him away with a clear warning: "If your shoes ever get you here again, I shall have you hanged . . . with the shoes around your neck!"

Isn't it terrible, all this happening to Tanboury? His old shoes are giving him no end of trouble. And *what* trouble! And really, all he has been trying to do is to get rid of his old, dirty, twisted, patched, worthless shoes. Yet no matter how he does it, they always manage to come back to him.

Poor Tanboury! Moaning and groaning with pain, he could hardly drag himself back to his hut in the *khan*. His old shoes were so heavy that they pulled his body to one side. What was worse, everyone was jeering at him.

"Behold," people said, "how faithful are Tanboury's shoes! They won't leave him for anything in the world! If only people were as faithful to each other."

And poor Tanboury hung his head in shame, although he would have liked to cry out: "It is not the fault of my shoes, you fools! Blame those who insist on bringing them back to me."

Once more that night Tanboury could not close his eyes. His back was so sore from the flogging that he had to sleep on his stomach. He went to bed without food, so great was his pain, and he did not even light a candle, so heavy was his misery. He doubted whether he would be able to get up in the morning. But at dawn there came the noise of men and animals on the square outside the *khan,* followed by banging on the gate.

Tanboury had no choice. He dragged himself from bed and went downstairs, moving slowly to spare his aching limbs. He unlocked the gate and drew it wide open, then shuffled back to his hut and gingerly went back to bed.

Now he fell into a deep slumber, and awoke only at nightfall. His body was still aching, but hunger was also gnawing at him. He lit a candle, brought out some food and sat on his bed to eat it. As he ate, his brain began to clear.

He looked at his old shoes in the doorway; they seemed to be taunting him. Tanboury rose and began pacing back and forth, thinking, thinking. Then, late in the night, a wonderful idea came to him. He decided to take action at once. He picked up his old shoes, took the candle, and went down to the deserted courtyard of the *khan*. From the tool shed in the corner he chose a spade, then selected a soft spot in the courtyard and began to dig. He dug and dug and did not stop until he had dug a pit half as deep as a man's height. Then he picked up his shoes, raised them high above his head, and slammed them into the pit. This done, he leaned on the spade and smiled happily. Now the shoes will be gone forever! He shoveled the soft earth back into the pit, stamping on it to

pack it down firmly. The stamping became a dance of joy, and Tanboury hummed a merry tune with each step. He went back to his hut, unmindful of the pain in his body.

Is Tanboury back in bed? Good! Let us leave him there and move quietly to the edge of the *khan* roof. Carefully we lean over the stone railing and peer into the darkness of the square on the other side of the wall. Nothing seems to be stirring but, on the other side of the gate, while Tanboury was digging the pit, someone's eye was at the keyhole watching what was going on inside the yard.

Aha! Now that our eyes have become accustomed to the darkness, we can even see who the peeper is! He is one of the merchants, who came to the *khan* much too early. He first propped himself up against the wall for a short nap before dawn. When he heard the sound of digging inside, he crept to the keyhole and peeked through. He could not see exactly what it was Tanboury was doing but, very suspicious by nature and always on the lookout to catch someone doing something wrong, he was sure that Tanboury was digging the pit to cover up some crime he had committed. When he saw Tanboury throw something into the pit, he was sure of it. As soon as dawn broke, he left his camels with his helpers and hurried off to see his kinsman, the Police Chief of Baghdad.

The Chief had heard about Tanboury and the trouble he had been giving the Governor. When he heard the merchant's story, he clapped his hands with delight. This was his chance to show how well he was guarding the city. He would also shame the Governor, who had been bossing him too much lately. The Chief immediately sent policemen to the *khan,* along with a crew of diggers, giving them orders to remove everyone from the yard, and dig, dig, dig!

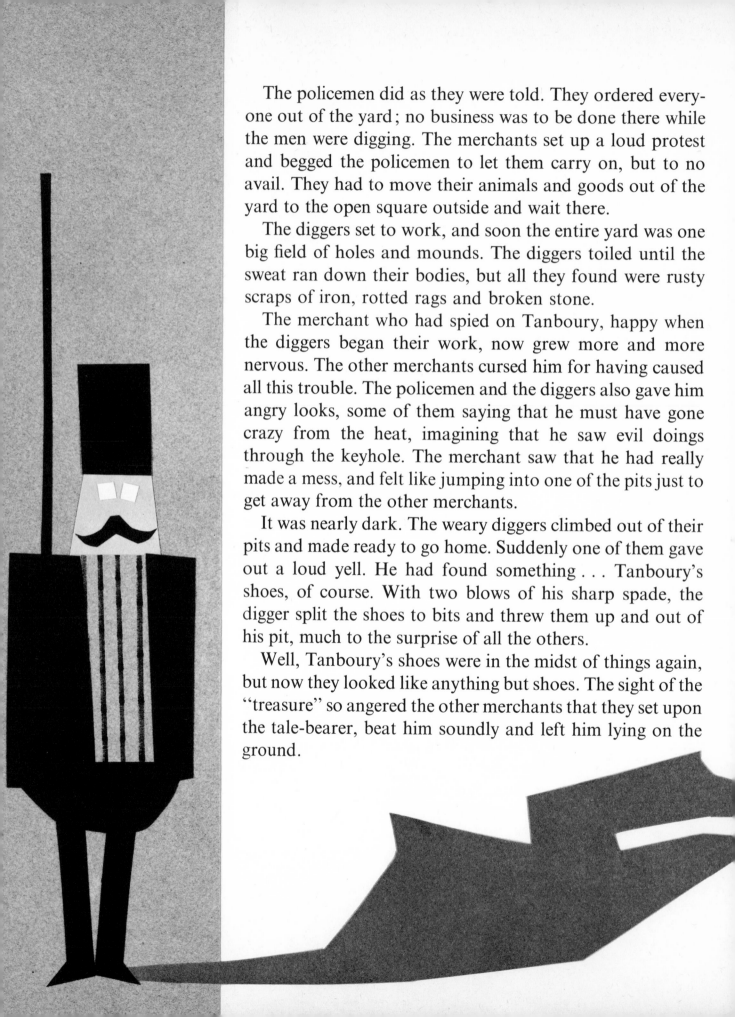

The policemen did as they were told. They ordered every-one out of the yard; no business was to be done there while the men were digging. The merchants set up a loud protest and begged the policemen to let them carry on, but to no avail. They had to move their animals and goods out of the yard to the open square outside and wait there.

The diggers set to work, and soon the entire yard was one big field of holes and mounds. The diggers toiled until the sweat ran down their bodies, but all they found were rusty scraps of iron, rotted rags and broken stone.

The merchant who had spied on Tanboury, happy when the diggers began their work, now grew more and more nervous. The other merchants cursed him for having caused all this trouble. The policemen and the diggers also gave him angry looks, some of them saying that he must have gone crazy from the heat, imagining that he saw evil doings through the keyhole. The merchant saw that he had really made a mess, and felt like jumping into one of the pits just to get away from the other merchants.

It was nearly dark. The weary diggers climbed out of their pits and made ready to go home. Suddenly one of them gave out a loud yell. He had found something . . . Tanboury's shoes, of course. With two blows of his sharp spade, the digger split the shoes to bits and threw them up and out of his pit, much to the surprise of all the others.

Well, Tanboury's shoes were in the midst of things again, but now they looked like anything but shoes. The sight of the "treasure" so angered the other merchants that they set upon the tale-bearer, beat him soundly and left him lying on the ground.

Just then Tanboury arrived, carrying a package of food. He was feeling fine until he entered the yard and saw what was going on. His eyes almost popped out of his head, and the parcel fell from his hands. And now the people in the yard knew what the digger had found. They threw bits and patches of leather at Tanboury, and the entire *khan* echoed with their laughter.

The only one who did not join in the merriment was the police officer in charge of the diggers. He went up to Tanboury, laid his heavy hand on the poor watchman's shoulders, and said: "You are under arrest. Come with me to the Police Chief." His gruff voice did not make Tanboury feel any better, either.

When the Chief heard the report, he was terribly disappointed. He sat and racked his brain for some way to deal with Tanboury in a manner that would save his own honor. He finally decided to throw Tanboury into the dungeon for a long stretch of time so that people would think that he had really done something criminal.

And so, without so much as a trial or a chance to defend himself, Tanboury was thrown into the dungeon. It is quite likely that our poor friend would have ended his days there, since he was poor and lonely and without a soul to speak for him at the Caliph's court. But help came to Tanboury in quite a strange way.

As we know, there was bad feeling between the Governor of Baghdad and the Police Chief. Perhaps we should add that these two officials let no chance go by to cause each other as much trouble as they could. The Chief had thrown Tanboury into jail to show that he was doing a better job of protecting the city than was the Governor.

Now the Governor saw his chance to put the Chief in his place, once and for all. Strange, isn't it? Only a few days earlier the Governor had ordered Tanboury flogged, and now he actually demanded that Tanboury be set free immediately!

The Governor called all the important men of Baghdad to his mansion. The Police Chief, he told them was falling down on his job. Instead of seeing to it that the citizens and their homes were kept safe from real criminals, he was arresting and jailing innocent people, merely to make a lot of noise and impress everyone. "Imagine," said the Governor, "a stupid merchant comes to his relative, the Police Chief, with a cock-and-bull story, and at once the Chief orders the entire *khan* dug up and all business stopped. This can ruin the name of the city! And then what does this smart Police Chief do? He grabs a poor man, a loyal citizen, the faithful watchman of the *khan,* and throws him into the dungeon, ignoring the fact that the *khan* and everything stored in it would be left open to the winds! And mind you," continued the Governor, "what crime did this man commit? He merely tried to bury his old shoes, so that they would not get him into trouble again. And for this he is being punished, so harshly and unjustly!"

The Governor did not stop there. He sent for the merchants and the caravan drivers, and they told the gathering in the mansion about the harm that the Chief's action had caused to their trade. At this, all the people in the mansion agreed that word should be sent to the Caliph himself, asking him to look into the matter. The Caliph called the Governor, and this gentleman told the powerful Caliph, ruler of all the

people, all about the case. The Caliph listened, then sent for the Police Chief. The Chief came and threw himself at the Caliph's feet, but it did him no good. The Caliph ordered him stripped of his rank and branded publicly as a faithless man. The Caliph then issued another decree, appointing the Governor as Police Chief also.

And that is how our friend Tanboury, once a poor and miserable man, suddenly found fortune smiling upon him. Even the Caliph was told what a fine fellow Tanboury was. Needless to say, Tanboury was released from the dungeon in time to hear the herald proclaim in the market place that the Police Chief had been replaced.

We should add that when the jailkeeper came to tell Tanboury that he was free, the poor man did not believe his ears. Even when he was out in the open air, walking about in his red shoes wherever he pleased, he still could not believe it. He kept pinching himself, as he gazed at the houses, the trees, his shoes. He breathed deeply of the pure air and blinked in the bright sunshine after all those days in the dark, foul dungeon.

He walked about Baghdad all day, as though he had never seen the city before in his life. Towards evening he went back to the *khan*. The merchants gave him a rousing welcome, and the caravan drivers cheered and cheered. Everyone was happy because Tanboury was free.

And Tanboury's old shoes? Believe it or not, people began saying that there was some kind of magic in those shoes: first they got Tanboury into trouble, then they got him out of trouble. Tanboury himself believed every word of it. He gathered up the bits, cleaned them and sewed them together again, then he placed them in his hut. Many a night he looked at them and thought of all the strange events that had befallen him because of them.

Many, many years went by. Tanboury, the faithful watchman of the *khan,* grew old and died, Allah rest his soul. The new watchman threw all of Tanboury's things out of the hut, the famous shoes among them, and no one in Baghdad ever saw them again.

Later, the old *khan* itself crumbled into ruin and the camel caravans no longer stopped there. Baghdad itself was overthrown by the enemies of the Caliph, and an end came to its palaces and gardens and mosques and towers. The rulers of the city were no more, but among the simple people the story of Tanboury and his shoes was not lost.

It was written into the thick books of Baghdad history, and that is how we know about the shoes of Tanboury today.

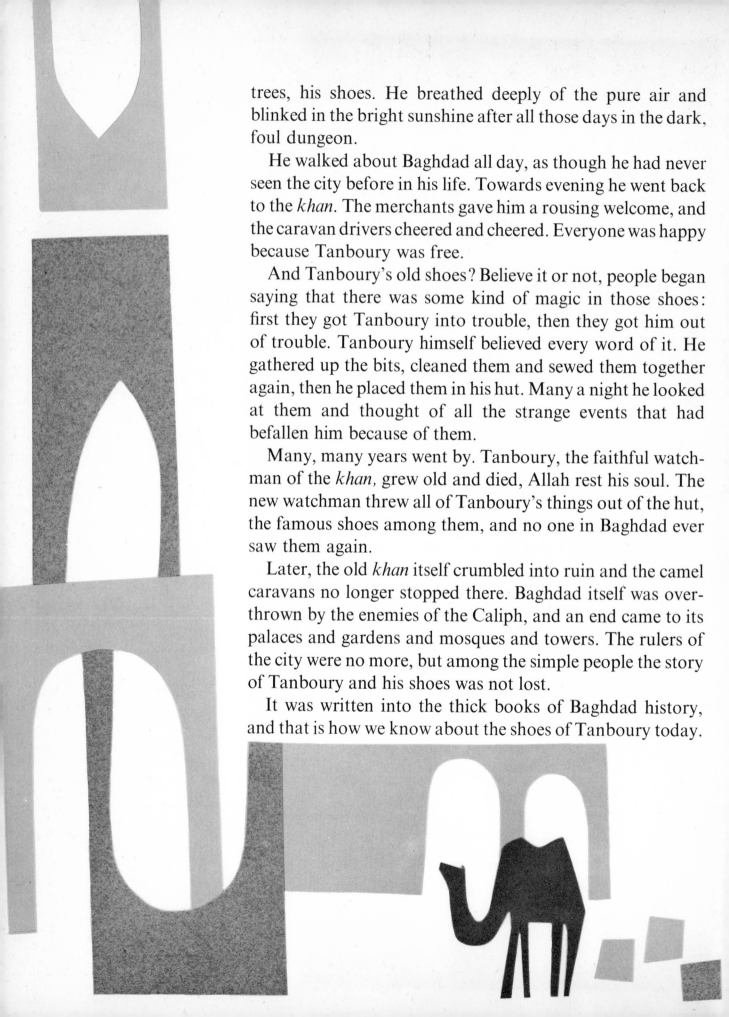